MAGNETISM
& MAGNETS

MICHAEL FLAHERTY

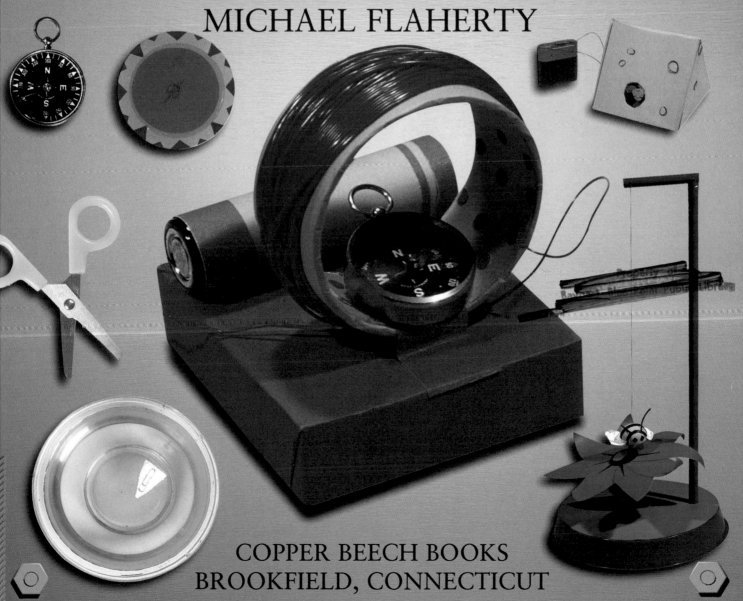

COPPER BEECH BOOKS
BROOKFIELD, CONNECTICUT

© Aladdin Books Ltd 1999

Designed and produced by
Aladdin Books Ltd
28 Percy Street
London W1P 0LD

First published in the United States
in 1999 by
Copper Beech Books,
an imprint of
The Millbrook Press
2 Old New Milford Road
Brookfield, Connecticut 06804

Design
David West
Children's Book Design

Designer
Flick Killerby

Illustrator
Ian Moores

Printed in Belgium

Cataloging-in-Publication Data is on
file at the Library of Congress.

ISBN 0-7613-3257-X (lib. bdg.)

1 3 5 4 2

The author, Michael Flaherty, has
written a number of science and
nature books for children.

The consultant, Steve Parker, has
worked on over 150 books for
children, mainly on a science theme.

All the photos in this book were
taken by Roger Vlitos.

INTRODUCTION

Magnetism and Magnets looks at the basic aspects of magnetism, as well as its more complex and practical uses. By following the projects, the readers are able to develop their practical skills, while at the same time expanding their scientific knowledge. Other ideas then offer them the chance to explore each aspect further to build up a more comprehensive understanding of the subject.

CONTENTS

YOUR FACTORY

BEFORE YOU START any of the experiments, it is important that you learn a few simple rules about the care of your science factory.

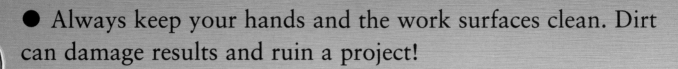

● Always keep your hands and the work surfaces clean. Dirt can damage results and ruin a project!

● Read the instructions carefully before you start each project.

● Make sure you have all the equipment you need for the project (see checklist opposite).

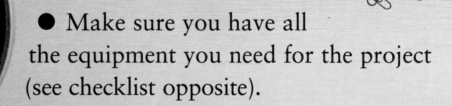

● If you don't have the right piece of equipment, then improvise. For example, a dish detergent bottle will do just as well as a plastic drink bottle.

● Don't be afraid to make mistakes. Just start again — patience is very important!

Equipment checklist:
- Scissors, adhesive tape, and glue
- Magnets of many shapes
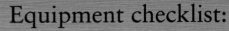
Magnetic and nonmagnetic objects
Plastic bottle, sticks, and sand
Paints and polystyrene
Flower pot tray and shallow dish
Sand and iron filings
Colored paper and cardboard
Modeling clay
Batteries
Coins and washers
- Paper clips and thumbtacks
- Drinking straw
- Compasses
- Table-tennis balls
- Needles, iron nails, and corks
Pencil and spool
Insulated wire

WARNING:
Some of the experiments in this book need the help of an adult. Always ask a grown-up to give you a hand when you are using sharp objects, like nails, or electrical objects!

METALS AND MAGNETS

MANY SUBSTANCES ARE METALS, such as iron, aluminum, copper, and gold. But only a few metals are magnetic — able to attract and repel other magnetic substances. The main magnetic metal is iron. Treasure hunters use magnetic metal detectors to find magnetic metallic objects. Build your own metal detector in the project below.

WHAT YOU NEED

Cardboard
Glue
Stick
Button magnet
Modeling clay
Flower pot tray full of sand
Colored paper
Magnetic and nonmagnetic objects

HIDDEN TREASURE

1 *Cut out a cardboard circle 4 inches (10 cm) across and cut a slit from the edge to the center. Overlap and glue the two ends to make a cone. Push the end of a stick through the center for a handle. Attach a button magnet inside the cone with modeling clay.*

2 *Wind strips of paper around the stick and glue them to the cone to hold it in place. Decorate the cone with colored strips of paper.*

WHY IT WORKS

A magnet is made up of tiny magnetic parts called domains that are all pointing in the same direction. Other metals also have domains, but they point in many different directions. A magnet makes the domains in ferrous (iron-based) metal line up. The metal becomes magnetized.

DIFFERENT MAGNETIC DOMAINS

3 Cover the bottom of a shallow flower pot tray with sand. Bury some magnetic and some nonmagnetic objects in the sand.

MAGNETIC MATERIALS

Collect as many different materials as you can find. First guess which ones you think are magnetic and which ones aren't. Then test them against a magnet. Were you right? Did any of the objects surprise you?

4 Move your metal detector slowly over the sand. Hold it at different heights to discover how low to hold it to find objects.

MAGNETIC FIELDS

EVERY MAGNET HAS AREAS WHERE ITS MAGNETIC FORCE IS STRONGEST. These areas are called poles. Every magnet has at least two poles, depending on its shape. The poles are named north and south. Surrounding every magnet is a magnetic field. This is created by lines of force going between the poles. This project shows you these lines of force.

WHAT YOU NEED
Two bar magnets
Large sheet of paper
Iron filings

FIELD EXPERIMENT

WHY IT WORKS

Lines of magnetic force run from pole to pole. They are strongest near the poles, where they are closest together. The iron filings are drawn to the magnetic field and show the lines of force. They concentrate around the poles where the lines of force meet.

NORTH

SOUTH

LINES OF FORCE

1 *Ask a grown-up to make some iron filings by filing down an iron nail. Now scatter them over the surface of the paper.*

FIELD PATTERNS

You can repeat this experiment with as many differently shaped magnets as you can find. How do their field patterns vary? Try to guess the shape of the magnetic field of a magnet by the shape of the magnet itself.

2 Place two bar magnets in line on a table top between two books. Lay the paper across the two books over the magnets. Tap the paper and watch the iron files line up along the magnetic fields.

PUSHING AND PULLING

WHEN TWO METAL OBJECTS PULL, or attract, each other it is difficult to tell if both of them are magnets. The real test is to see if they push, or repel, each other. The south pole of one magnet seeks the north pole of another magnet and repels the other's south pole. Test this out in the bumblebee project below.

WHAT YOU NEED

Button magnet
Bar magnet
Colored paper
Paints
Modeling clay
Sticks
Flower pot tray
Table-tennis ball
Glue

BUMBLEBEE

1 Ask an adult to cut a table-tennis ball in half. Paint the outside with the black and yellow stripes of a bee. Add some paper wings, eyes, and feelers.

2 Place a button magnet inside the bee using modeling clay, with one of its poles facing down.

3 Glue two sticks together to make a frame. Make a hole in an upside-down flower pot tray and insert the longer stick. Hold it firmly in place with some modeling clay.

4 Cover a bar magnet in brown paper for the stem of the flower. Stand it upright in the center of the base with modeling clay, with the pole that repels the bee on top.

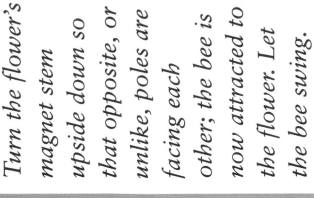

ZOOMING IN

Turn the flower's magnet stem upside down so that opposite, or unlike, poles are facing each other; the bee is now attracted to the flower. Let the bee swing. How long does it swing?

5 Cut out some petals from colored paper and make a large flower. Attach it to the top of the bar magnet stem.

6 Suspend the bee from the frame with a piece of thread.

7 Swing the bee over the flower and watch it buzz around the flower. Does it ever come to rest?

WHY IT WORKS

The poles facing each other in this project are the same, or like, poles; they strongly repel each other. This makes the bee swing for a very long time because the flower is pushing the bee away all the time. Only two magnets can repel each other like this.

REPEL
SOUTH
NORTH
NORTH
SOUTH
NORTH
SOUTH
NORTH
ATTRACT
SOUTH
SOUTH
NORTH

HOMEMADE MAGNET

YOU CAN MAKE YOUR OWN MAGNETS FROM NEEDLES AND PAPER CLIPS. Then you can test them by seeing if they attract and repel one another (see the project on pages 10-11). Magnets made from iron slowly lose their magnetic effect over time. Magnets made from steel are permanent magnets.

see the project on pages 10-11

WHAT YOU NEED
Needle
Paper clip
Shallow dish
Styrofoam
Magnet

MAKING A MAGNET

1 *Stroke one end of a paper clip with the south pole of a magnet, at least twenty times. Always stroke the paper clip in the same direction, and lift it well clear at the end to start a new stroke. This end will be the north pole of the paper clip.*

2 *Tape the paper clip to a piece of styrofoam shaped like a boat with the north pole pointing towards the front. Float it in a shallow dish of water.*

WHY IT WORKS

Magnets push and pull each other because opposite poles attract one another and like poles repel one another. This attraction and repulsion is strong enough to move the styrofoam boat through the water. When the north pole of the needle is brought close to the north pole of the paper clip, the paper clip is pushed away. This force is so strong it is sometimes almost impossible to push two magnets together.

3 Stroke the eye of the needle with the north pole of the magnet. This magnetizes the needle, making the eye the south pole of the needle and the point the north pole.

4 Bring the eye of the needle near the end of the paper clip. The front of the boat turns toward the needle.

5 Turn the needle around and bring its point near the end of the paper clip. The boat turns away from the needle.

BOUNCING MAGNETS

Place a piece of wood between two magnets with like poles on top of each other. Tape the magnets together and remove the wood. The two magnets repel each other, but the tape keeps them in place. Press down on the top magnet and see it spring back or twist because of the repulsion. This is how a Maglev (magnetic levitation) train works (see page 31).

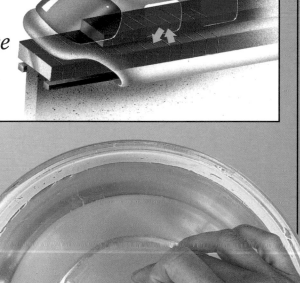

TRAVELING MAGNETISM

MAGNETIC FORCE CAN TRAVEL THROUGH MANY MATERIALS, EVEN WATER. Divers use an instrument called a magnetometer to uncover treasure on the ocean floor. You have seen a magnetic field travel through paper to iron filings (see pages 8-9). What other materials do you think magnetic fields can travel through? This project shows that magnetism is not stopped by nonmagnetic materials.

WHAT YOU NEED
Colored cardboard
Two sticks
Table-tennis ball
Two bar magnets
Two small magnets
Cardboard lid
Adhesive tape

CORK BOBBING

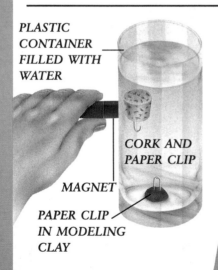

PLASTIC CONTAINER FILLED WITH WATER

CORK AND PAPER CLIP

MAGNET

PAPER CLIP IN MODELING CLAY

Cut the top off a plastic bottle. Attach a paper clip to the bottom. Fill the bottle with water. Push a paper clip into a cork to make a hook. Use a bar magnet to drag the cork beneath the water and hook it to the paper clip at the bottom.

MAGNETIC HOCKEY

1 Cut out two cardboard figures holding hockey sticks. Paint them with team colors. Tape a magnet onto each hockey stick.

2 Tape bar magnets to the end of two long sticks for moving your players. Check that the poles of the magnets attract one another.

3 Make the rink from an upside-down cardboard lid. Set the lid on four wooden legs. Make the goals out of strips of cardboard. Mark the center with colored tape or paint.

WHY IT WORKS

Some nonmagnetic materials allow magnetic force to pass through them without being affected. Magnets on either side of a piece of cardboard still attract or repel each other. The thicker the material or the further apart the magnets are, the weaker the magnetic force.

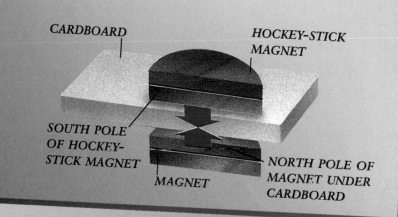

CARDBOARD

HOCKEY-STICK MAGNET

SOUTH POLE OF HOCKEY-STICK MAGNET

MAGNET

NORTH POLE OF MAGNET UNDER CARDBOARD

4 Place the players on the "ice" and move them using the sticks with the magnets under the ice. Use a table-tennis ball to score goals.

MAGNETIC EARTH

THE EARTH BEHAVES LIKE A GIANT MAGNET. It produces a magnetic field and has two poles. Its magnetic poles are not in exactly the same place as its true poles. A compass needle has been magnetized and points to the earth's magnetic north pole. In the project below you can show how the earth acts as a big magnet.

WHAT YOU NEED
Colored cardboard
Five compasses
Bar magnet
Glue

ORIENTEERING

Orienteering means finding your way across the land with a map and a compass. The compass needle points to magnetic north. As you read your map you have to make an adjustment to your compass reading to find true north.

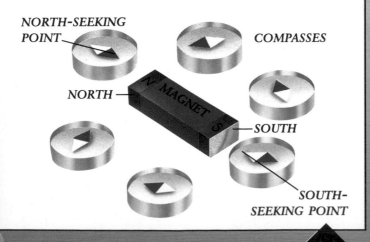

NORTH-SEEKING POINT

COMPASSES

NORTH

SOUTH

SOUTH-SEEKING POINT

FROM POLE TO POLE

1 Cut out a circle of blue cardboard. Draw the map of the world onto cardboard of a different color. Stick it onto the blue circle. This is your earth.

2 You will need five compasses to lay around the outside of your map.

3 Lay the bar magnet under your map, with the north pole at the top and the south pole at the bottom.

WHY IT WORKS

The needles of the compasses follow the lines of magnetic force of the bar magnet. The same kind of field exists around the earth. In the top half of your map, the compass needles point to the north pole of the magnet and the miniature earth.

NORTH POLE

SOUTH POLE

4 Position each compass as shown here, with the north of the compass dial pointing north. The needles move to follow the lines of force of the bar magnet under your map.

COMPASS BEARINGS

WHAT YOU NEED
Shallow dish
Cork
Magnet
Steel needle

IN THE PREVIOUS PROJECT, WE SAW HOW THE EARTH ACTS LIKE A GIANT MAGNET. Chinese and Mediterranean sailors started to use magnetic compasses about 1,000 years ago. These first compasses were little more than magnetized pieces of iron floating on cork in bowls of water (see pages 12-13). You can make your own compass.

MAKE A COMPASS

1 *Half-fill a shallow dish with water. Magnetize a steel needle by stroking one end of a magnet along its length at least 50 times. Always stroke the needle in the same direction and lift it well clear of the magnet at the end to start a new stroke.*

ALTERNATIVE COMPASS

Any magnet or magnetized object will align itself with the earth's magnetic field if it is allowed to swing freely. You can make a different compass by balancing a magnetized needle on a fold of paper on top of an upright stick. Cover this delicate compass with a see-through container to keep any wind from blowing it off and it will swing around to seek north.

2 *Ask an adult to push the needle through a cork. Float the cork in the water, making sure it balances evenly. As the water becomes still again, the needle will swing around to seek the earth's magnetic north pole.*

WHY IT WORKS

Stroking the needle with a magnet lines up all the domains in the needle, and it becomes magnetized. In the water, the needle is free to move and aligns itself with the earth's magnetic field.

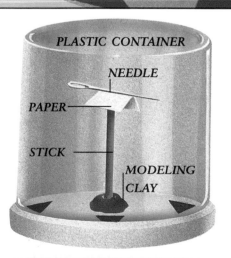

PLASTIC CONTAINER

NEEDLE

PAPER

STICK

MODELING CLAY

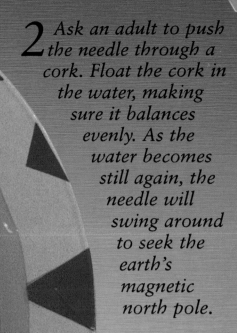

DIRECTION OF STROKE

PERMANENT MAGNET

SECTION OF UNMAGNETIZED NEEDLE

SECTION OF MAGNETIZED NEEDLE

ELECTROMAGNETS

THE RELATIONSHIP BETWEEN ELECTRICITY AND MAGNETISM WAS DISCOVERED IN THE 1800s. The Danish physicist, Hans Christian Oersted discovered that an electric current running through a wire produces a magnetic field. By coiling the wire around a soft iron bar, the iron bar becomes magnetized as long as the current is running through the wire. This is called an electromagnet.

MORE POWER

Increase the power of your electromagnet. Wrap the insulated wire around the nail at least sixty times. Attach the battery and see what you can now pick up. Add another battery and see what effect this has. How long does the battery last?

WHY IT WORKS

An electromagnet is made by coiling an insulated wire around an iron core, like an iron nail. An electric current flowing through the wire creates a magnetic field around the iron core. This causes the domains in the piece of iron to line up in the same direction, turning it into a magnet.

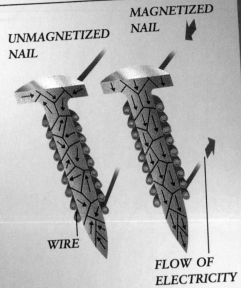

UNMAGNETIZED NAIL

MAGNETIZED NAIL

WIRE

FLOW OF ELECTRICITY

ELECTROMAGNETIC CRANE

1 Make the crane out of two boxes. Make the arm of the crane from cardboard. Attach a spool inside the arm with a pencil. Wind insulated wire around the nail at least twenty-five times. Thread both ends of the wire down the arm.

3 When the paper clip touches both thumbtacks, the circuit is complete and the current flows. This turns the nail into an electromagnet, which can pick up metal objects.

2 Attach one end of the wire to a battery terminal in the crane. Attach the other end to a thumbtack in the side of the crane. Attach a paper clip to this tack, to make a switch. Push another tack into the side of the crane and attach it to the other battery terminal by a wire.

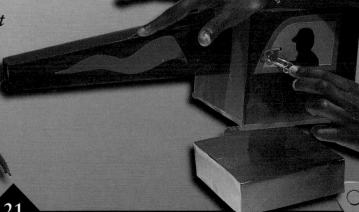

MAGNETS AND MOTION

WHAT YOU NEED
Cardboard
Battery
Insulated wire
Drinking straw
Needle
Modeling clay

IN THE 1800S, WHEN ELECTROMAGNETS WERE FIRST INVENTED, people discovered that they could also make things move using electromagnetism. This is done by using a coil of wire wrapped around a tube, called a solenoid. Solenoids are used in switches, such as some doorbells. Make your own solenoid and watch the mouse duck into the cheese.

2

Coil a piece of insulated wire around a plastic drinking straw. Place it on some modeling clay inside the cheese wedge, opposite the hole. Make a small hole in the triangular door and thread the ends of the wire through it.

PEEKING MOUSE

1

Cut out three squares and two triangles of cardboard to make a wedge of cheese. Make a hole in one of the squares for the mouse to peek out of. Make sure one of the sides can be opened and closed.

WHY IT WORKS

The current running through the wire produces a magnetic field. This field is made stronger because the wire is coiled close together. The needle is attracted to the magnetic field and is pulled inside the coil.

3

Make a mouse's face from paper, and attach it to the end of the needle with modeling clay. Make sure the mouse's head fits through the hole.

4

Slide the needle into the straw, leaving the mouse peeking out of the hole. Connect the wire to a battery and watch the mouse.

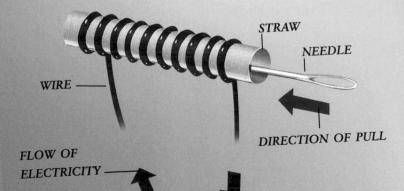

STRAW

NEEDLE

WIRE

DIRECTION OF PULL

FLOW OF ELECTRICITY

MAGNETS AND MOTORS

AFTER SCIENTISTS FOUND THEY COULD MAKE THINGS MOVE WITH MAGNETISM (see pages 22-23), British scientist Michael Faraday produced continuous motion by passing an electric current through a metal wire in a strong magnetic field. He developed a forerunner of the electric motor in 1821. You can produce continuous motion in this project by getting a compass needle to spin.

WHAT YOU NEED
Two batteries
Adhesive tape
Cardboard tube
Paper
Insulated wire
Compass

2 *Wrap insulated copper wire at least fifty times around a short, wide cardboard tube. Leave the two ends of the wire free to connect to the batteries.*

SPINNING COMPASS

1 *Place two batteries end to end so that opposite terminals are touching. Wrap them in paper to keep them together.*

3 *Attach the coil of wire to a base with adhesive tape. Attach the batteries to the base in the same way.*

WHY IT WORKS

The current turns the coil into an electromagnet and attracts the compass needle. When the current is turned on and off rapidly, the compass needle spins around. An electric motor works on this principle.

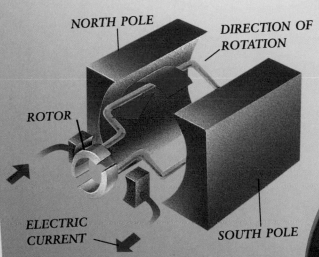

NORTH POLE

DIRECTION OF ROTATION

ROTOR

ELECTRIC CURRENT

SOUTH POLE

MAKING A CURRENT

A magnet moving near a coil of wire creates an electric current in the wire. This is called a dynamo. Where can you find dynamos? Some bicycle lights are run on a dynamo attached to the bicycle's wheels.

4 Place a compass inside the coil. Connect the wires to the ends of the batteries and see what happens to the compass needle. Now repeatedly connect and disconnect one of the wires to the battery and see what happens to the compass needle.

MAKING CURRENT

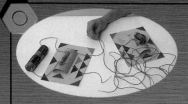

WHAT YOU
NEED
*Cardboard
tube
Insulated wire
Compass
Adhesive tape
Iron nail
Battery*

In 1831, both British scientist Michael Faraday and American physicist Joseph Henry discovered that moving a magnet through a coiled wire causes an electric current to flow through the wire. Soon the induction coil was developed, where a varying current flowing through one coil of wire causes a current to flow through a second coil of wire within a magnetic field. Make an induction coil for yourself.

INDUCTION COIL

1 *Wrap a length of insulated wire fifty times around a large iron nail. Secure each end with adhesive tape to keep the coil from unwinding. Leave about 4 inches (10 cm) free at each end of the wire so you can attach it to a battery.*

2 *Over the first coil, wrap the middle section of the second piece of wire fifty times in the opposite direction and secure with sticky tape.*

3 *Wrap a third piece of wire about thirty times around a compass and connect its ends to the ends of the second piece of wire so that the compass can sit about 3 feet (1 m) away from the coiled nail. This is to prevent the nail from directly affecting the compass.*

4 *Make holders for the compass and the nail out of flattened cardboard tubes and squares of cardboard.*

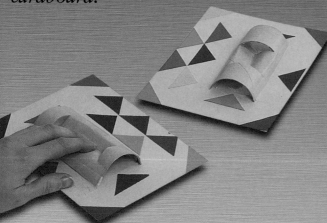

5 *Connect one end of the first wire to a battery terminal. Touch the other end of the wire to the other battery terminal, repeatedly switching the current on and off. The compass needle will swing back and forth every time you do this.*

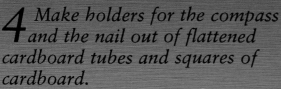

WHY IT WORKS

Because the current in the first coil is constantly interrupted, it causes its own magnetic field to change all the time. This changing magnetic field creates an electrical field in the second coil, causing a current to flow. Induction only works when the current is changing.

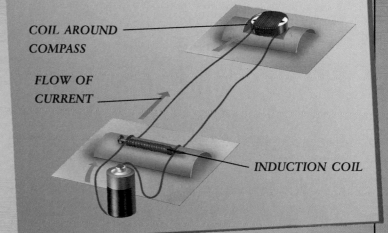

COIL AROUND COMPASS

FLOW OF CURRENT

INDUCTION COIL

VOLTAGE

Put more turns into the second coil. This increases the strength, or voltage, generated in the second coil. What happens to the compass needle?

MAGNETS IN MACHINES

Magnets and electromagnets are used in many machines in the home and in industry and science. Weak magnets hold refrigerator and cupboard doors shut. Powerful magnetic fields hold or move atoms in a machine called a particle accelerator, which smashes the atoms to pieces. Machines like ticket machines at the train station use magnets to sort out coins. Make your own slot machine to sort out your coins.

WHAT YOU NEED
Stiff cardboard
Magnet
Adhesive tape
Coins
Washers

WHY IT WORKS

When you drop coins and washers into the machine, they go down the ramp passing by the magnet. Anything magnetic, such as the steel washers and the coins of some countries, are attracted to the magnet and swing to the right, collecting in the right side of the tray at the bottom. Nonmagnetic coins and washers are unaffected and roll into the left side of the tray.

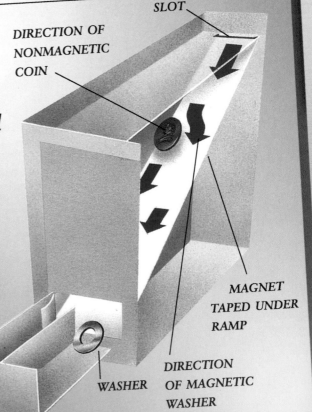

SLOT

DIRECTION OF NONMAGNETIC COIN

MAGNET TAPED UNDER RAMP

WASHER

DIRECTION OF MAGNETIC WASHER

SLOT MACHINE

1 Attach a strong magnet to the underside of a length of cardboard. Make sure it is on the right-hand side of the cardboard.

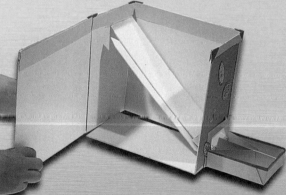

2 Fit the cardboard diagonally inside a tall box to make a ramp, as shown. Hinge one side of the box so you can open and close it. Cut a hole in the side of the box at the bottom of the ramp and attach a tray divided in two.

3 Seal the top of the box with a piece of cardboard. Cut a slot in this lid on the opposite side to the ramp's magnet.

4 Collect as many different coins and metal washers as you can find and drop each one into the slot machine through the slot in the lid.

WEATHER FORECASTING

Draw a map of the U.S. and attach it to a magnetic surface like the refrigerator. Cut weather symbols out of cardboard and attach magnets to them. Give weather forecasts by putting your symbols on the map.

COMPASS A tool for showing direction, using a magnetic needle that can turn freely to point to magnetic north. *Make a compass in the project on pages 18-19.*

DOMAIN Any of the tiny magnetic regions of a magnet or magnetic metal. *The project on pages 6-7 shows you how to make these domains line up to magnetize a metal.*

ELECTROMAGNET A magnet created by an electric current running through a wire wrapped around an iron core. *See pages 20-21 to make your own electromagnet.*

INDUCTION COIL The electromagnetic field created by a changing current flowing through a wire coil will cause a current to flow in a second coil.

SPECTRUM

Electromagnetic waves include light and X rays. They have an electric field and a magnetic field.

MAGNETOSPHERE

The earth's magnetic field, called the magnetosphere, protects us from dangerously charged particles from the sun. Particles that get through the magnetosphere react with the atmosphere and appear as aurorae in the night sky.

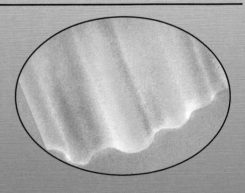

POLES

The earth's magnetic poles do not always stay in the same place. Over time they slowly wander (below) and have even completely swapped over many times.

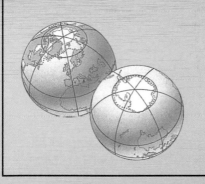

Set up an induction coil in the project on pages 26-27.

LINES OF FORCE

Imaginary lines within a magnetic field curving from the north pole to the south pole of a magnet. *Map these lines of force in the project on pages 8-9.*

MAGNETIC FIELD

The space around a magnet where it has magnetic influence. Magnetic objects in this magnetic field are pulled toward the magnet. *The project on pages 8-9 introduces you to the magnetic field.*

POLES Areas on a magnet or the earth where the lines of force are closest together and the magnetic field is strongest. *Find out how many poles different-shaped magnets have in the project on pages 8-9.*

SOLENOID A coil of wire wrapped around a cylinder. When a current flows through the wire, it acts like a magnet. Solenoids are used in switches and relays. *See how a solenoid works on pages 22-23.*

FLOATING TRAINS

Some trains float above their tracks by using electromagnets that repel each other. They are called magnetic levitation, or Maglev, trains.

INDEX